# THE POWER OF ESG INVESTING

# THE POWER OF ESG INVESTING

## NAVIGATING ENVIRONMENTAL, SOCIAL, AND GOVERNANCE FACTORS FOR SUSTAINABLE AND RESPONSIBLE INVESTING

### SOCIALLY RESPONSIBLE INVESTING

### ROBERT BUCKLEY

Book
Bound Studios

# PRAISE FOR ROBERT BUCKLEY

**From** *"The Power of ESG Investing:"*

The author does an excellent job of explaining complex financial concepts in a clear and accessible manner, making it an ideal resource for both seasoned investors and those new to the world of investing.

— STOICPRENEUR

I recently read "The Power of ESG Investing" and was thoroughly impressed. The authors do an excellent job of explaining the concept of Environmental, Social, and Governance (ESG) investing and its growing significance in the investment world. The book provides a clear and concise overview of the key ESG factors to consider when making investment decisions, along with practical advice for incorporating ESG considerations into an investment strategy.

— MARK VAN

For anyone wanting to know more about ESG investing, and why considering ESG factors is important, this book is a must read! Well written & chapter summaries make the information easy to digest.

— R MURRELL

*To my family for their unwavering support and encouragement throughout the writing of this book. And to my mentor and friend Justina, whose guidance and wisdom have been invaluable in shaping my understanding of ESG investing.*

The future is something which everyone reaches at the rate of sixty minutes an hour, whatever he does, whoever he is.

— C.S LEWIS

# CONTENTS

# $10.99 FREE EBOOK

**Receive Your Free Copy of The Power of Intelligent Investing**

Or visit:
bookboundstudios.wixsite.com/robert-buckley

# INTRODUCTION

Environmental, social, and governance (ESG) investing has gained significant attention in recent years as more investors have become interested in aligning their investments with their values. ESG investing is a type of investing that incorporates consideration of a company's environmental, social, and governance practices and performance into investment decisions. The purpose of this chapter is to provide an overview of ESG investing, including its definition, the growing popularity of ESG investing, and the goals and benefits of incorporating ESG considerations into investment decisions. We will also explore the various environmental, social, and governance considerations that investors should consider when evaluating a company's ESG practices and performance. This chapter aims to provide a comprehensive introduction to ESG investing, setting the stage for a deeper dive into the following topic in the subsequent chapters.

## Definition of ESG Investing

ESG investing, or environmental, social, and governance investing, is a type of investment strategy that incorporates consideration of a company's environmental, social, and governance practices and performance into investment decisions. Environmental factors include a company's environmental impact, such as its carbon footprint and approach to natural resources management. Social factors include a company's labor practices, community engagement, and its approach to diversity, equity, and inclusion. Governance factors include a company's management structure, board composition, executive compensation, lobbying approach, advocacy, and transparency. ESG investing is also known as sustainable, responsible, or impact investing.

ESG investing involves evaluating a company's impact on the environment, its treatment of employees, customers, and communities, and how it manages and governs itself. This type of investing is gaining popularity among investors who want to align their investments with their values and **contribute to a more sustainable future.** ESG investors are looking to achieve financial returns while promoting positive social and environmental change by investing in companies committed to sustainable business practices. By considering a company's ESG practices and performance, investors can identify potential risks and opportunities that may not be reflected in traditional financial analysis. Additionally, ESG investing can help align investors' values with their investments, promote greater corporate accountability and transparency, and contribute to developing a more sustainable global economy.

## The Growing Popularity of ESG Investing

In recent years, ESG investing has gained significant attention and popularity among investors, becoming one of the fastest-growing investment trends. This is due to the growing awareness of the importance of sustainable practices and investors' role in promoting positive social and environmental change. The increasing focus on climate change and environmental sustainability, as well as the growing awareness of social and governance issues, has led many investors to re-evaluate their investment strategies and consider the impact of their investments on the world around them.

Several factors have contributed to the growing popularity of ESG investing. One of the main drivers has been the increasing awareness of the urgent need for action on climate change and environmental sustainability. As the impacts of climate change become more severe and widespread, investors are increasingly recognizing the need to invest in companies that are taking action to reduce their carbon footprint and promote sustainable resource management.

Another factor has been the growing awareness of social and governance issues, such as labor practices, community engagement, and diversity and inclusion. Investors are becoming increasingly concerned about the companies' social and governance practices. As a result, they are looking for ways to invest in companies that promote positive social and environmental outcomes.

In addition to these external factors, there has also been a growing body of research that demonstrates the potential financial benefits of ESG investing. For example, several studies have shown that companies with strong ESG practices tend to have better management, lower risk, and higher long-term returns. This has led many investors to re-evaluate their investment strategies and consider the impact of their investments on the world around them.

The growing popularity of ESG investing has also been reflected in the **growing number of ESG-focused investment products and services.** For example, increasing numbers of asset managers and investment companies are launching ESG-focused funds and products, and many index providers are developing ESG-focused indices and benchmarks. This has made it easier for investors to access ESG-focused investment opportunities, further driving the popularity of ESG investing.

## The Goals and Benefits of ESG Investing

The primary goal of ESG (environmental, social, and governance) investing is to achieve financial returns while promoting positive social and environmental change. This approach to investing seeks to identify companies with strong financial performance and demonstrate a commitment to sustainable business practices. By considering a company's ESG practices and performance, investors can identify potential risks and opportunities that may not be reflected in traditional financial analysis. Additionally, ESG investing can help align investors' values with their investments, promote greater corporate accountability and transparency, and contribute to developing a more sustainable global economy.

The benefits of ESG investing are numerous. One of the main benefits is that companies with strong ESG practices tend to have better management and lower risk, which can result in **higher long-term returns**. This is because companies with a strong commitment to sustainable business practices are more likely to have better governance, more transparent operations, and more efficient use of resources, which can lead to long-term financial performance.

ESG investing can also help to mitigate risks associated with climate change, labor practices, and other social and environmental issues. For example, investing in companies committed to reducing their carbon footprint and promoting sustainable resource management can help mitigate the financial risks associated with climate change. Similarly, investing in companies with strong labor practices and promoting diversity and inclusion can help mitigate the risks associated with social and governance issues.

ESG investing can also promote the development of more sustainable business practices. Investing in companies committed to sustainable business practices can create a financial incentive to continue improving their environmental, social, and governance practices. Additionally, by engaging with companies on ESG issues, investors can help promote greater corporate accountability and transparency, leading to more sustainable business practices.

All in all, ESG investing is a powerful tool that can help investors achieve financial returns while promoting positive social and environmental change. By considering a company's ESG practices and performance, investors can identify potential risks and opportunities that may not be reflected in traditional financial analysis, align their values with their investments, promote greater corporate accountability and transparency, and contribute to developing a more sustainable global economy.

In conclusion, ESG investing is a rapidly growing trend in the investment world, driven by increasing awareness of the importance of sustainable practices and investors' role in promoting positive social and environmental change. By considering a company's ESG practices and performance, investors can identify potential risks and opportunities that may not be reflected in traditional financial analysis. Additionally, ESG investing can help align investors' values with their investments, promote greater corporate accountability and transparency, and contribute to developing a more sustainable global economy. In the next chapter, we will delve deeper into environmental considerations in ESG investing, including climate change and baron emissions, renewable energy and resource efficiency, and biodiversity and habitat preservation.

# 1

## ENVIRONMENTAL CONSIDERATIONS IN ESG INVESTING

This chapter will explore how environmental factors play a crucial role in socially responsible investing. We will delve into five topics that are particularly relevant in today's sustainable investing landscape: climate change and carbon emissions, renewable energy and resource efficiency, biodiversity and habitat preservation, water management, and pollution control, and waste management and recycling programs. We aim to comprehensively understand how these environmental factors impact investment decisions and how investors can use this knowledge to make informed and responsible choices. We hope this chapter will serve as a valuable resource for those interested in responsible investing and its impact on our planet.

### Climate Change and Carbon Emissions

Climate change is one of our most significant environmental challenges, and it profoundly impacts the planet and the global economy. Burning fossil fuels, deforestation, and other human activities have increased greenhouse gas emissions, causing global temperatures to rise and resulting in more extreme weather events, rising sea levels, and other negative environmental impacts. As a result, climate change poses a significant risk to the global economy, and companies **must** take action to reduce their carbon footprint and mitigate the risks associated with climate change.

*A tree with its roots firmly planted in the ground representing the foundation of ESG investing.*

One of the key ways that companies can reduce their carbon footprint is by reducing their greenhouse gas emissions. Companies can achieve this through various methods, such as investing in renewable energy, implementing energy-efficient practices, and using clean technology. In addition, companies committed to reducing their greenhouse gas emissions are more likely to be sustainable in the long term and, therefore, are more attractive to ESG investors.

Another way to mitigate the risks associated with climate change is by investing in renewable energy and clean technology. Renewable energy sources such as solar, wind, and hydropower produce no emissions, and they help to reduce the use of fossil fuels, which are a major contributor to climate change. Clean technology, on the other hand, refers to technology that is designed to reduce environmental impact. Therefore, investing in companies developing and deploying renewable energy and clean technology can help mitigate the risks associated with climate change and promote sustainable development.

Lastly, ESG investors are increasingly looking to divest from companies that rely heavily on fossil fuels. As the world shifts towards cleaner energy sources, companies heavily dependent on fossil fuels are becoming more vulnerable to stranded assets, regulatory risks, and reputational risks. By divesting from these companies, investors can mitigate the risks associated with climate change and promote sustainable development.

In conclusion, climate change and carbon emissions are major environmental challenges that pose significant risks to the global economy. As a result, ESG investors are increasingly looking to invest in companies that are taking action to reduce their carbon footprint and mitigate the risks associated with climate change.

## Renewable Energy and Resource Efficiency

The importance of utilizing renewable energy sources and implementing resource efficiency practices cannot be overstated when achieving sustainable development. Renewable energy, such as solar and wind power, does not generate harmful emissions and helps to reduce our dependence on fossil fuels, which are major contributors to climate change. On the other hand, resource efficiency involves sustainably using resources with minimal waste, which can greatly reduce the environmental impact of our actions, lower costs, and increase overall efficiency.

Companies committed to utilizing renewable energy sources and implementing resource efficiency practices are more likely to be **sustainable in the long term.** As a result, they are better positioned to be competitive in the future energy market. This has led to an increased interest from ESG investors in such companies, as they can provide benefits such as reduced risk, improved financial performance, and long-term sustainability.

By investing in companies that are actively working towards increasing renewable energy and resource efficiency, we can not only help to reduce the environmental impact of our actions but also benefit from the long-term sustainability of these companies. Therefore, individuals and organizations need to recognize the importance of renewable energy and resource efficiency in achieving sustainable development and take the necessary steps to promote and invest in these practices.

*A majestic wind turbine stands tall against a brilliant sunset symbolizing the limitless power of renewable energy.*

### Biodiversity and Habitat Preservation

Biodiversity and habitat preservation are critical for maintaining the health and resilience of the planet's ecosystems. Biodiversity refers to the variety of life on Earth, including plants, animals, and microorganisms that make up the planet's ecosystems. Habitat preservation refers to protecting and preserving natural habitats, such as forests, wetlands, and oceans, which are critical for maintaining biodiversity and supporting the planet's ecosystems.

The loss of biodiversity and habitat destruction is a major environmental issue that poses significant risks to the planet's ecosystems. Habitat destruction and loss of biodiversity can lead to the extinction of species, loss of ecosystem services, and increased vulnerability to natural disasters and climate change. It is, therefore, important that companies take action to protect and preserve biodiversity and habitats.

ESG investors are increasingly looking to invest in businesses committed to biodiversity and habitat preservation. This can include investing in companies committed to sustainable resource management, such as companies working to reduce their impact on natural habitats and ecosystems. For example, companies that practice sustainable forestry, fishing, and mining are less likely to cause damage to natural habitats and ecosystems. As a result, they are more likely to be sustainable in the long term. Additionally, investing in companies working to preserve and protect natural habitats and biodiversity can help mitigate the risks associated with habitat destruction and loss of biodiversity.

Another way that companies can support biodiversity and habitat preservation is by investing in conservation and restoration projects. This can include investing in reforestation projects, wetland restoration, and other initiatives that help to protect and preserve biodiversity and habitats.

All in all, biodiversity and habitat preservation are critical for maintaining the health and resilience of the planet's ecosystems. As a result, ESG investors are increasingly looking to invest in companies committed to biodiversity and habitat preservation. Investing in companies committed to sustainable resource management, conservation, and restoration projects, and preserving and protecting natural habitats and biodiversity can help mitigate the risks associated with habitat destruction and loss of biodiversity and promote sustainable development.

## Water Management and Pollution Control

Water management and pollution control are critical considerations for investing in environmental, social, and governance (ESG). As water is a **finite resource** and pollution can significantly negatively impact human health and the environment, companies that effectively manage and reduce their water usage and pollution can be considered more sustainable investments.

Water management involves the responsible use and conservation of water resources. This includes reducing water usage through efficient practices, implementing recycling and reuse systems, and protecting water sources from pollution. Companies with strong water management practices can reduce their environmental footprint and save on water procurement and treatment costs.

On the other hand, pollution control involves reducing the release of harmful substances into the environment, including water. This includes reducing the use of hazardous chemicals, implementing proper disposal methods for waste materials, and monitoring for and preventing spills and leaks. As a result, companies with strong pollution control practices can protect the environment and human health and reduce the risk of legal and reputational damage.

When evaluating companies for ESG investing, it is important to look at their water management and pollution control practices. This can include analyzing their water usage and conservation efforts, reviewing their environmental impact reports and sustainability goals, and assessing their compliance with relevant laws and regulations. It is also important to consider the company's industry, as certain industries may have a higher potential for water usage and pollution.

Investors can also consider investing in companies specializing in water management and pollution control technologies and services. These companies can provide solutions for other companies to improve their water management and pollution control practices. They can also benefit from increased demand for sustainable water management and pollution control solutions.

In conclusion, water management and pollution control are important considerations for ESG investing. Companies with strong water management and pollution control practices can be considered more sustainable investments. Investors can also consider investing in companies specializing in water management and pollution control technologies and services.

## Waste Management and Recycling Programs

Waste management and recycling programs are crucial components of environmental, social, and governance (ESG) investing. These programs help protect the environment and generate economic and social benefits for communities and businesses.

Effective waste management and recycling programs involve the collection, transportation, and processing of waste materials in a manner that reduces their environmental impact. This can include reducing waste in landfills, increasing materials recycling, and finding new uses for waste products.

One key aspect of waste management and recycling programs is diverting waste from landfills. Landfills are a significant source of greenhouse gas emissions and can negatively impact air and water quality. By diverting waste from landfills through recycling and composting, we can greatly reduce the environmental impact of waste.

Another important aspect of these programs is the recycling of materials. Recycling conserves natural resources, reduces energy consumption and the need for new landfills, and can create jobs and economic benefits. In addition, many materials, such as paper, glass, and metal, can be recycled multiple times, making them a valuable resource.

*A bustling city street lined with colorful recycling bins overflowing with paper, plastic, and glass.*

Many companies are looking for innovative ways to use waste as a resource. This is commonly known as a circular economy. As a result, companies can benefit from cost savings, reduced waste, and improved environmental performance.

Furthermore, ESG investors should consider the environmental performance of companies in the waste management and recycling industry. They should assess the environmental impact of the company's operations, its compliance with environmental regulations, and efforts to reduce waste and promote recycling. Investors can also look for companies developing new technologies and processes to improve waste management and recycling.

Overall, waste management and recycling programs are important aspects of ESG investing. These programs can help to protect the environment, generate economic and social benefits, and create new business opportunities. ESG investors can support these programs by investing in companies committed to effective waste management and recycling practices and implementing circular economy strategies.

In conclusion, this chapter has highlighted the importance of considering environmental factors in ESG investing. From climate change and carbon emissions to waste management and recycling programs, we have explored how these factors play a crucial role in sustainable investing. We hope this chapter has provided a comprehensive understanding of how these environmental factors impact investment decisions and how investors can use this knowledge to make informed and responsible choices. In the next chapter, we will delve deeper into social considerations in ESG investing, including labor practices, community engagement, diversity, equity, inclusion, product safety, and consumer protection.

## Chapter Summary

- Climate change and carbon emissions are major environmental challenges that pose significant risks to the global economy.
- Companies can reduce their carbon footprint by investing in renewable energy, implementing energy-efficient practices, and using clean technology.
- ESG investors are increasingly looking to invest in companies that are taking action to reduce their carbon footprint and mitigate the risks associated with climate change.
- Renewable energy and resource efficiency are important for achieving sustainable development.
- Biodiversity and habitat preservation are critical for maintaining the health and resilience of the planet's ecosystems.
- Companies must take action to protect and preserve biodiversity and habitats.
- Water management and pollution control are important considerations for ESG investing.
- Waste management and recycling programs help protect the environment and generate economic and social benefits for communities and businesses.

# SOCIAL CONSIDERATIONS IN ESG INVESTING

This chapter delves into the crucial topic of evaluating and addressing social issues in ethical and sustainable investing. The chapter aims to provide readers with a comprehensive understanding of the various social considerations that should be considered when evaluating investments from an ESG perspective. The chapter will explore four key areas of social responsibility: labor and human rights, community engagement and development, diversity, equity, and inclusion, and product safety and consumer protection. By examining these topics, the chapter will provide readers with a framework for assessing and addressing social considerations in their investment decisions. Overall, this chapter will serve as a valuable resource for investors looking to incorporate social considerations into their ESG investing strategies.

## Labor and Human Rights

ESG investing focuses on labor and human rights. Investors are looking for companies that treat their workers fairly and ethically, provide safe and healthy working conditions, and improve their supply chain. This can lead to long-term benefits for investors.

*A weary factory worker stands amidst the chaos of machinery.*

When companies are committed to labor and human rights, it can lead to many positive outcomes. It can also lead to a more socially responsible and ethical investment portfolio. This can be particularly important for those looking to align their investments with their values.

Moreover, companies with good labor and human rights record tend to have better employee retention, lower recruitment cost, and more loyal customers, which can lead to higher productivity, better financial performance, and sustainable growth. Therefore, ESG investing, which puts labor and human rights as critical components, can also help investors achieve their financial goals while doing good for society.

Overall, ESG investing is a way for investors to take a more holistic approach. By focusing on labor and human rights, they can promote fair treatment of workers, positively impact the local communities, contribute to a more sustainable global economy, and achieve their financial goals.

## Community Engagement and Development

Community engagement and development are also important components of social considerations in ESG investing. This includes ensuring that a company is engaged with the communities in which it operates and is committed to promoting the development and well-being of these communities. Companies that do not engage with their communities and do not contribute to their development can face **significant** reputational, legal, and financial risks. Additionally, it can also lead to a negative impact on the company's ability to attract and retain employees and customers. Finally, it can also lead to a negative impact on the local communities where they operate.

ESG investors are increasingly looking to invest in companies committed to community engagement and development. This can include investing in companies that have strong community engagement policies and are committed to promoting the development and well-being of the communities in which they operate. This can include training and education programs, supporting local charities and community organizations, and investing in community development projects.

Additionally, investors can invest in companies committed to contributing to the development of local communities through philanthropy and other initiatives. This can include providing financial support to local charities, volunteering with local organizations, and supporting local entrepreneurs. Furthermore, companies committed to community engagement and development are more likely to positively impact the local communities where they operate, which can lead to long-term sustainability.

In conclusion, community engagement and development are important components of social considerations in ESG investing. Investing in companies committed to community engagement and development can promote the development and well-being of the communities in which they operate and contribute to the long-term sustainability of the company and the local community. This can lead to long-term financial benefits for investors and contribute to a more sustainable global economy.

*A bustling farmer's market in a vibrant community where locals gather to shop for fresh produce and connect with their neighbors.*

## Diversity, Equity, and Inclusion

Diversity, equity, and inclusion have increasingly become focal points for socially conscious investors in environmental, social, and governance (ESG) investing. These considerations are crucial for ensuring that a company is committed to promoting and fostering a culture of diversity, equity, and inclusion in all aspects of its operations, from the workplace to its interactions with customers, suppliers, and other stakeholders.

Failing to promote and maintain a diverse and inclusive environment can have significant consequences for a company, including reputational risks, legal and financial repercussions, and potentially even a loss of customers or investors. As such, ESG investors are becoming more discerning and are looking to invest in companies that demonstrate a commitment to diversity, equity, and inclusion.

One way to do this is by investing in companies that have implemented strong policies and initiatives to promote diversity, equity, and inclusion in the workplace, including programs that support underrepresented groups and provide training and education on these issues. Additionally, investors can look for companies committed to promoting diversity, equity, and inclusion in their supply chains and the communities in which they operate, as well as those with a track record of supporting and partnering with organizations that advocate for diversity and inclusion.

In short, investing in companies that prioritize diversity, equity, and inclusion aligns with the values of socially conscious investors. Moreover, it mitigates potential reputational and financial risks for the company. As such, it is becoming an increasingly important consideration for ESG investors.

## Product Safety and Consumer Protection

Environmental, social, and governance (ESG) investing is a rapidly growing field that focuses on the impact of a company's actions on the environment, society, and governance. One important aspect of ESG investing is evaluating a company's commitment to product safety and consumer protection.

Product safety refers to the measures a company takes to ensure that its products are free from defects and are not harmful to consumers. On the other hand, consumer protection refers to how a company ensures that consumers are not misled or taken advantage of in the marketplace.

When evaluating a company's commitment to product safety and consumer protection, investors should consider factors such as the company's history of product recalls, compliance with industry regulations, and transparency in disclosing product-related information to consumers.

One important consideration for investors is a company's history of product recalls. Companies with a history of recalling products due to safety concerns may be at a higher risk for future recalls, leading to financial losses and damaging the company's reputation.

Another important consideration is a company's compliance with industry regulations. Companies that are found to be non-compliant with industry regulations may be at a higher risk of facing penalties and fines, which can also lead to financial losses.

Investors should also consider a company's transparency in disclosing product-related information to consumers. Companies that are transparent in their product labeling and marketing practices are more likely to be trusted by consumers, which can lead to long-term financial success.

Overall, evaluating a company's commitment to product safety and consumer protection is an important aspect of ESG investing. Companies prioritizing these issues are more likely to be responsible corporate citizens and more likely to be **financially successful** in the long term.


In conclusion, this chapter has provided an in-depth examination of the social considerations that should be considered when evaluating investments from an ESG perspective. The chapter has explored labor and human rights, community engagement and development, diversity, equity, and inclusion, and product safety and consumer protection as key areas of social responsibility that investors should consider when making investment decisions. By understanding and addressing these social considerations, investors can make more informed decisions that align with their values and contribute to a more sustainable and just society.

As we have seen, social considerations are essential to ESG investing. However, they are not the only component. Governance considerations, such as a company's management structure and ethical practices, also play a crucial role in determining an investment's overall sustainability and ethicality. Therefore, the next chapter will delve into governance considerations in ESG investing and provide a framework for evaluating and addressing these considerations in your investment decisions. By understanding and addressing environmental, social, and governance considerations, investors can make ethical and sustainable investment decisions that align with their values and contribute to a more just and equitable society.

## Chapter Summary

- ESG investing focuses on labor and human rights, community engagement and development, diversity, equity, inclusion, product safety, and consumer protection.
- Companies prioritizing labor and human rights tend to have better employee retention, lower recruitment costs, and more loyal customers.
- Companies committed to community engagement and development are more likely to positively impact the local communities where they operate.
- Diversity, equity, and inclusion are important social considerations in ESG investing.
- Product safety and consumer protection are important aspects of ESG investing.
- Companies with a history of product recall and non-compliance with industry regulations may be at a higher risk of facing financial losses.
- Companies that are transparent in their product labeling and marketing practices are more likely to be trusted by consumers.
- Understanding and addressing environmental, social, and governance considerations is essential for ethical and sustainable investment decisions.

# 3

## GOVERNANCE CONSIDERATIONS IN ESG INVESTING

This chapter will explore the various governance considerations crucial in environmental, social, and governance (ESG) investing. The topics covered in this chapter include corporate governance and executive compensation, transparency and disclosure, political lobbying and advocacy, anti-corruption and bribery policies, and tax transparency and responsible tax practices. These topics are essential for understanding corporate governance's impact on a company's performance and sustainability and how it affects investment decision-making. This chapter aims to provide readers with a comprehensive understanding of the governance considerations central to ESG investing and how we can use them to evaluate potential investments. Overall, this chapter will provide readers with the knowledge and tools necessary to make informed investment decisions based on governance considerations within the ESG framework.

### Corporate Governance and Executive Compensation

Corporate governance is vital to managing and operating a company effectively and efficiently. It refers to the set of rules, practices, and processes that are put in place to ensure that a company is properly directed and controlled. Good corporate governance is essential for creating an environment where a company can thrive and succeed.

Good corporate governance is important not only for a company's internal operations but also for external stakeholders. ESG investing is a growing trend in the investing world, and good corporate governance is **crucial** to this type of investing. ESG investors are looking at a company's financial performance and considering its impact on the environment, society, and the way it governs itself. A company with strong corporate governance is more likely to be well-managed, accountable, and responsive to the needs of its stakeholders. This can lead to better financial performance and greater stability over the long term, which is beneficial for both the company and its investors.

*A close-up shot of a large ornate desk with a stack of papers a pen and a calculator sitting on top.*

In addition to the financial benefits, good corporate governance also helps to promote ethical behavior and integrity within a company. It helps to ensure that a company is run with transparency, fairness, and accountability, which can foster trust and confidence among stakeholders. This can lead to a positive reputation for the company, which can be beneficial in attracting and retaining customers, employees, and investors.

Executive compensation is an important aspect of corporate governance that investors should carefully consider. The amount of compensation paid to executives can provide insight into the level of alignment between management and shareholders. High levels of executive compensation may be a sign that the interests of management are not aligned with the interests of shareholders and that the company is not being run in the best interests of its stakeholders.

Investors should look at executive compensation when evaluating a company and compare it to industry standards and peers. They should also consider the company's performance and whether the compensation levels are commensurate with its financial results. If executive compensation is high, it may signify a need for greater alignment between management and shareholders.

In addition to evaluating executive compensation levels, investors should also look for companies that have adopted governance practices that align the interests of management with those of shareholders. This can include practices such as providing shareholders with an advisory vote on executive compensation, having independent directors on the board, and implementing performance-based compensation. These practices ensure that the company's management maximizes value for all stakeholders rather than just themselves.

Overall, corporate governance is essential to a company's effective and efficient management. It involves a set of rules, practices, and processes that ensure a company is properly directed and controlled. Good corporate governance is important not only for a company's internal operations but also for external stakeholders. It is crucial for ESG investing, a growing trend in the investing world. Companies with strong corporate governance are more likely to be well-managed, accountable, and responsive to the needs of their stakeholders, leading to better financial performance and greater stability over the long term. Additionally, good corporate governance promotes ethical behavior and integrity within a company, fostering trust and confidence among stakeholders. Investors should carefully evaluate executive compensation levels and look for companies that have adopted governance practices that align the interests of management with those of shareholders.

**Transparency and Disclosure**

Transparency and disclosure are critical elements in ensuring proper corporate governance. These concepts are paramount for investors, as they clearly understand a company's operations, financial performance, and potential risks. In addition, this level of transparency and disclosure allows investors to make informed decisions based on accurate and up-to-date information and helps to build trust between a company and its investors.

Companies that demonstrate a strong commitment to transparency and disclosure are generally considered to be better governed than those that do not. This is because **transparency and disclosure are key indicators** of a company's commitment to ethical and responsible business practices. In addition, by providing investors with detailed information about the company's operations and performance, companies can demonstrate their commitment to being accountable for their actions.

Moreover, transparency and disclosure also play a vital role in building trust between a company and its stakeholders. When companies are open and transparent in communicating with investors, they are more likely to be viewed as trustworthy and responsible corporate citizens. This, in turn, can improve the company's overall reputation and enhance its standing in the business community.

Overall, transparency and disclosure are essential components of good corporate governance. By providing investors with accurate and up-to-date information about the company's operations and performance, companies can demonstrate their commitment to ethical and responsible business practices and help to build trust between the company and its investors. This ultimately leads to a more responsible and sustainable corporate culture, which benefits all stakeholders.

## Political Lobbying and Advocacy

Regarding governance considerations, political lobbying and advocacy play a crucial role. Companies that engage in these activities have the potential to shape public policy and regulations significantly. This is why it is essential for investors to be aware of a company's lobbying and advocacy efforts and to evaluate whether they align with their values and investment goals.

Lobbying is the act of attempting to influence decisions made by government officials, primarily legislators and members of regulatory agencies. Businesses can do this through direct communication with legislators, grassroots campaigns to mobilize public support, or funding third-party organizations that advocate for specific policies. Conversely, advocacy is publicly supporting or opposing a particular issue or policy.

Companies engage in lobbying and advocacy for various reasons. For example, they may seek to influence regulations that directly affect their business, such as environmental laws or taxes. They may also seek to shape broader policy issues that indirectly impact their operations, such as healthcare or trade policy.

While lobbying and advocacy can benefit companies, they can also have negative consequences. For example, a company that lobbies for policies that harm the environment or undermine workers' rights may be seen as unethical by some investors. Additionally, a company that spends significant money on lobbying may be viewed as diverting resources away from more productive uses.

In light of these considerations, investors should be aware of a company's lobbying and advocacy activities and assess whether they align with their values and investment goals. Investors can do this by researching a company's lobbying spending and agenda and looking into the company's public statements and advocacy efforts. By taking these steps, investors can make more informed decisions about the companies they invest in.

### Anti-Corruption and Bribery Policies

Anti-corruption and bribery policies are essential elements of good governance. They are increasingly being recognized as important considerations in responsible and sustainable investing. This section will explore the risks and opportunities associated with corruption and bribery in environmental, social, and governance (ESG) investing.

First, it is important to understand the scope of the problem. Corruption and bribery are pervasive issues affecting virtually every sector and region worldwide. According to the World Bank, corruption costs the global economy **$2 trillion annually**. In addition to financial costs, corruption and bribery undermine the rule of law, erode trust in institutions, and lead to human rights violations.

For investors, the risks associated with corruption and bribery include reputational damage, legal and regulatory enforcement actions, and reduced financial performance. For example, companies that engage in corrupt or bribery practices may be subject to fines, penalties, and legal action, leading to significant financial losses for investors. In addition, companies that are known to be involved in corruption or bribery may find it more difficult to access capital markets and may face increased scrutiny from regulators, rating agencies, and other stakeholders.

However, there are also opportunities for investors who take a proactive approach to address corruption and bribery risks in their portfolios. For example, many companies have implemented anti-corruption and anti-bribery policies and procedures to mitigate these risks. As a result, these companies may be better positioned to navigate the legal and regulatory landscape. As a result, they may be more attractive to investors looking for companies that prioritize good governance.

ESG investors can take several steps to identify and mitigate corruption and bribery risks in their portfolios. These include:

- Incorporating anti-corruption and anti-bribery considerations into investment analysis and decision-making processes.

- Engaging with companies to understand their policies and practices related to corruption and bribery and encouraging them to adopt best practices in this area.
- Collaborating with other investors and stakeholders to promote transparency and accountability in the companies they invest in.
- Monitoring and reporting on companies' performance regarding anti-corruption and anti-bribery policies and practices.

In conclusion, anti-corruption and anti-bribery policies are essential elements of good governance and responsible investing. Investors should be aware of the risks associated with corruption and bribery and take steps to identify and mitigate them in their portfolios. By promoting transparency, accountability, and good governance, ESG investors can help to create a more sustainable and responsible global economy.

## Tax Transparency and Responsible Tax Practices

As environmental, social, and governance (ESG) investing grows, responsible tax practices are increasingly important focus areas for investors and companies. This includes compliance with local and international tax laws and transparency and fairness in how taxes are paid and reported.

One key aspect of tax transparency is the ability of investors to understand a company's tax footprint. This includes information on where and how much the company is paying in taxes and any potential tax avoidance or evasion practices. Unfortunately, this information can be difficult to obtain, as many companies keep this information private. However, investors can use several resources, such as the Tax Justice Network's Financial Secrecy Index, to better understand a company's tax practices.

Another important aspect of responsible tax practices is the concept of *"fair tax."* This refers to the idea that companies should pay their fair share of taxes in the countries where they operate and earn profits. This can include measures such as avoiding tax havens, paying taxes at a rate commensurate with the company's level of profits, and avoiding aggressive tax planning strategies.

In addition to the above, responsible tax practices also include compliance with local and international tax laws and not engaging in any illegal activities related to taxes. Many companies today have tax policies that ensure compliance with all laws and regulations, which is important for protecting the company and its investors.

*An open book on a wooden desk with a pen resting on top beside it a calculator and a stack of papers.*

As investors increasingly focus on ESG factors, companies need to be transparent and responsible in their tax practices. This can build trust with investors and contribute to long-term financial success.

Overall, tax transparency and responsible tax practices are important aspects of ESG investing. Investors can use resources to understand a company's tax practices better. Companies should be transparent and responsible in their tax practices to build trust with investors and contribute to long-term success.

. . .

In conclusion, this chapter has examined the various governance considerations crucial in environmental, social, and governance (ESG) investing. We have explored corporate governance and executive compensation, transparency and disclosure, political lobbying and advocacy, anti-corruption and bribery policies, and tax transparency and responsible tax practices. These topics are essential for understanding corporate governance's impact on a company's performance and sustainability and how it affects investment decision-making. The information presented in this chapter has highlighted the importance of considering governance considerations as a fundamental aspect of the ESG investment process. Understanding and evaluating these considerations allows investors to make more informed and responsible investment decisions.

With the knowledge gained in this chapter, readers are now equipped to move on to the next chapter, *"Integrating ESG Considerations into Investment Strategy."* This next chapter will build on the information presented in this book by providing practical examples and strategies for incorporating ESG considerations into an overall investment strategy.

**Chapter Summary**

- Corporate governance is essential to a company's effective and efficient management and is important for ESG investing.
- Good corporate governance promotes ethical behavior and integrity within a company, fostering trust and confidence among stakeholders.
- Transparency and disclosure are essential components of good corporate governance, allowing investors to make informed decisions based on accurate and up-to-date information.
- Political lobbying and advocacy can benefit companies but can also have negative consequences if they do not align with investors' values and investment goals.
- Anti-corruption and bribery policies are essential elements of good governance and responsible investing.

- Investors should be aware of a company's lobbying and advocacy activities and assess whether they align with their values and investment goals.
- Tax transparency and responsible tax practices are important aspects of ESG investing.
- Understanding and evaluating governance considerations allows investors to make more informed and responsible investment decisions.

# 4

## INTEGRATING ESG CONSIDERATIONS INTO INVESTMENT STRATEGY

Environmental, social, and governance (ESG) considerations are increasingly important in the investment world. As more investors recognize the potential risks and opportunities associated with these issues, many are looking for ways to integrate ESG considerations into their investment strategies. This chapter will explore three key approaches to integrating ESG considerations into investment strategy: screening and exclusion, active ownership and engagement, and impact investing.

### Screening and Exclusion

Screening and exclusion is a well-established method for integrating environmental, social, and governance (ESG) considerations into investment strategies. The process involves identifying companies or sectors that do not meet specific ESG criteria and subsequently excluding them from an investment portfolio. This approach is particularly useful for investors seeking to minimize potential risks associated with ESG issues while aligning their investments with their values.

One of the key aspects of screening and exclusion is identifying companies or sectors that do not meet the ESG criteria. Investors can do this through various methods, such as publicly available data on environmental performance, social impact, or governance practices or by engaging third-party ESG rating agencies. Once the companies or sectors that do not meet the ESG criteria have been identified, they can be excluded from the portfolio. This helps to ensure that the portfolio is composed of companies aligned with the investor's values and goals.

For example, investors may exclude companies with poor environmental records, such as those identified as major polluters or involved in environmental controversies. Similarly, investors may exclude companies involved in controversial business practices, such as those associated with human rights abuses or corruption. By excluding these companies, investors can **minimize the potential risks** associated with these issues and align their investments with their values.

In addition to minimizing potential risks, screening and exclusion can help investors capitalize on opportunities associated with ESG issues. For instance, by excluding companies with poor environmental records, an investor may be able to invest in companies that are leaders in sustainable practices, potentially leading to better long-term financial performance. Similarly, by excluding companies with poor governance practices, an investor may be able to invest in companies with strong corporate governance structures, potentially leading to better financial performance.

In conclusion, screening and exclusion is a well-established method for integrating ESG considerations into investment strategies. By identifying and excluding companies or sectors that do not meet specific ESG criteria, investors can minimize potential risks associated with ESG issues, align their investments with their values and capitalize on opportunities associated with ESG issues. Moreover, as the awareness and importance of ESG issues continue to grow, more investors will likely adopt this approach to integrate ESG considerations into their investment strategies.

## Active Ownership and Engagement

Active ownership and engagement is a powerful strategy for integrating environmental, social, and governance (ESG) considerations into investment decisions. This approach involves actively engaging with companies where an investor holds shares and encouraging them to improve their performance in areas related to ESG.

One key aspect of active ownership is using voting rights as shareholders to support or oppose resolutions related to ESG issues. For example, an investor may vote in favor of a resolution to reduce a company's carbon emissions or against a resolution that would weaken labor protections for workers. By using their voting rights in this way, investors can help to promote positive change within companies and encourage them to prioritize ESG considerations.

*A group of young business-people huddled around a bustling street-side café.*

Another important aspect of active ownership is direct engagement with company management. Investors can use this opportunity to discuss specific ESG issues with company leaders and encourage them to take action to improve their performance in these areas. For example, this might involve discussing reducing a company's environmental impact, improving labor practices, or increasing transparency and accountability. Through these engagements, investors can help to build a more sustainable and responsible corporate sector.

In addition to promoting positive change within companies, active ownership and engagement can also help enhance investors' long-term returns. By encouraging companies to prioritize ESG considerations, investors can help to build more sustainable and resilient businesses that are better positioned to navigate the challenges of the 21st century. This can ultimately lead to better financial outcomes for investors over the long term.

Overall, active ownership and engagement is a valuable approach for integrating ESG considerations into investment strategy and one that can help to promote positive change within companies and enhance long-term returns for investors.

**Impact Investing**

A third approach to integrating ESG considerations into investment strategy is *"impact investing."* This investment strategy involves directing capital toward companies, projects, or funds with a positive social or environmental impact. This approach to investing is based on the idea that financial returns and positive impact can go hand in hand. Investing in companies working towards solutions to pressing social and environmental issues, investors can achieve a financial return and contribute to creating a more sustainable and equitable world.

For example, an impact investor may choose to invest in a renewable energy company working to reduce greenhouse gas emissions or a company that provides affordable housing to low-income communities. These types of investments not only have the potential to generate financial returns but also provide a tangible positive impact on the world.

In addition to providing a way for investors to align their investments with their values, impact investing can offer several other benefits. For example, investments in sustainable and responsible companies may be less risky in the long term, as they are less likely to be impacted by negative social or environmental events. Impact investing can also help create jobs and economic opportunities in underserved communities.

Overall, impact investing is a powerful approach to integrating ESG considerations into an investment strategy. By investing in companies, projects, or funds with a positive social or environmental impact, investors can achieve a double bottom line of financial return and positive impact.

In conclusion, integrating ESG considerations into investment strategy is important for investors to manage potential risks and capitalize on opportunities associated with these issues. The approaches described in this chapter, including screening and exclusion, active ownership and engagement, and impact investing, can help investors to align their investments with their values and promote positive change in the world. As the awareness and importance of ESG issues continue to grow, more investors will likely adopt these and other approaches to integrate ESG considerations into their investment strategies.

## Chapter Summary

- Screening and exclusion is a well-established method for integrating ESG considerations into investment strategies, involving identifying and excluding companies or sectors that do not meet specific ESG criteria.
- Active ownership and engagement involve actively engaging with companies where an investor holds shares and encouraging them to improve their performance in areas related to ESG.
- Impact investing involves directing capital toward companies, projects, or funds with a positive social or environmental impact.
- Screening and exclusion can help investors minimize potential risks associated with ESG issues and align their investments with their values.
- Active ownership and engagement can help to promote positive change within companies and enhance long-term returns for investors.

- Impact investing can provide a way for investors to align their investments with their values and achieve a double bottom line of financial return and positive impact.
- Integrating ESG considerations into investment strategy is important for investors to manage potential risks and capitalize on opportunities associated with these issues.
- As the awareness and importance of ESG issues continue to grow, more investors will likely adopt these approaches to integrate ESG considerations into their investment strategies.

# 5

## MEASURING AND EVALUATING ESG PERFORMANCE

Measuring and evaluating the performance of environmental, social, and governance (ESG) factors is a crucial aspect of responsible investing. In this chapter, we will discuss the various methods of assessing ESG performance, including using ratings and indices and analyzing company-specific data. We will also address the limitations and challenges of ESG measurement.

### ESG Ratings and Indices

ESG, or environmental, social, and governance, is a term used to describe the three central factors that investors and analysts consider when evaluating a company's overall performance and potential for growth. One of the most widely accepted and recognized methods for measuring and evaluating a company's ESG performance is through the use of ratings and indices provided by third-party organizations.

These organizations, such as Sustainalytics, MSCI, and FTSE Russell, assess companies based on predefined criteria focusing on environmental impact, human rights, and corporate governance. These criteria are designed to provide a comprehensive and unbiased evaluation of a company's overall performance and potential for growth.

*MSCI ESG rating system demonstrating what it takes to become a laggard, average, or leader business. Source: MSCI*

Once a company has been assessed, it is given a rating or score that can be used to compare its performance to that of its peers. This allows investors and analysts to quickly and easily identify companies performing well in ESG and make more informed decisions about where to invest their money. Additionally, these ratings and indices can also be used by companies themselves to identify areas where they need to improve and to set goals for future performance.

Overall, ESG ratings and indices are valuable tools for investors, analysts, and companies, providing a clear and concise way to evaluate a company's performance and potential for growth in the long term. It is also an important tool for society to ensure sustainable development of society. Using ESG ratings and indices is becoming increasingly popular among investors and companies as they recognize the importance of considering ESG factors when making investment decisions. It helps promote sustainable and responsible business practices, which ultimately benefit society and the environment.

### Assessing Company-Specific ESG Data

Assessing company-specific environmental, social, and governance (ESG) data is crucial for measuring and evaluating a company's performance in these areas. This analysis includes an in-depth examination of various aspects of a company's operations, such as its carbon emissions, labor practices, and political lobbying. This information can be obtained from various sources, including a company's annual reports, sustainability reports, and other publicly available documents.

By analyzing this data, investors can gain a more detailed understanding of a company's ESG performance and identify areas for improvement. For example, an investor may find that a company has a high level of carbon emissions and decide to invest in a company with lower emissions. Similarly, an investor may find a company with poor labor practices and choose to invest in a company with better labor standards.

Furthermore, by assessing company-specific ESG data, investors can also compare the performance of different companies in the same industry. This can provide valuable insights into the industry's overall performance in terms of ESG and help investors make more informed investment decisions.

Additionally, assessing company-specific ESG data can help investors identify companies that are leaders in the field. These companies may be more likely to be successful in the long term as they are more likely to be responsive to the growing demand for sustainable and socially responsible investments.

In summary, assessing company-specific ESG data is essential for measuring and evaluating a company's performance in these areas. It allows investors to gain a more detailed understanding of a company's ESG performance, identify areas for improvement, compare the performance of different companies in the same industry and identify companies that are leaders in the field. This can assist investors in making more informed investment decisions.


## The Limitations and Challenges of ESG Measurement

The increasing use of environmental, social, and governance (ESG) measurements to assess companies' sustainability and ethical performance has brought several limitations and challenges to light. One of the most significant limitations is the need for more **standardized reporting and criteria** to evaluate ESG performance. This can make it challenging to compare the ESG performance of different companies, as there needs to be a clear, consistent framework for measurement.

*A team of scientists huddled around a large computer screen eagerly analyzing data and discussing their findings.*

Furthermore, there needs to be more transparency and reliability in the data that companies report, which can make it difficult to assess performance accurately. This is partly because there is no uniform method for collecting and reporting ESG data, which can lead to inconsistent or incomplete information. Additionally, Bad actors may incentivize companies to present their performance in the most favorable light, which can lead to biased or misleading data.

Another limitation is the need for more objective and comparable data in certain ESG areas, such as human rights or social factors, which can make it difficult to evaluate the performance of companies in these areas. Furthermore, the need for more consensus on what constitutes good performance in certain ESG areas, such as climate change or labor rights, can make it difficult to establish clear standards for measurement.

Overall, while the use of ESG measurement has grown in popularity, it is important to acknowledge these limitations and challenges to improve the accuracy and reliability of ESG assessments. Businesses can achieve this through more standardized reporting and criteria, increased data transparency and reliability, and addressing the need for more objective and comparable data in certain ESG areas.

· · ·

In conclusion, measuring and evaluating ESG performance is important for responsible investing. But, there are limitations and challenges, such as the need for standardization and transparency. Despite these challenges, assessing ESG performance is crucial for making informed investment decisions and promoting sustainable business practices.

**Chapter Summary**

- Measuring and evaluating environmental, social, and governance (ESG) performance is an important aspect of responsible investing.
- Ratings and indices provided by third-party organizations are widely accepted and recognized methods for assessing ESG performance.
- Companies can use these ratings and indices to identify areas for improvement and set goals for future performance.
- Assessing company-specific ESG data is also important for measuring and evaluating a company's performance in these areas.
- This data can be used to compare the performance of different companies in the same industry and identify companies that are leaders in the field.
- There are several limitations and challenges to ESG measurement, such as the need for more standardized reporting and criteria, increased data transparency and reliability, and more objective and comparable data in certain ESG areas.
- Despite these challenges, assessing ESG performance is important in making informed investment decisions and promoting sustainable business practices.
- Companies can address these challenges by implementing more standardized reporting and criteria, increasing data transparency and reliability, and addressing the need for more objective and comparable data in certain ESG areas.

# 6

# THE ROLE OF REGULATORS AND GOVERNMENT IN ESG INVESTING

As the world becomes increasingly focused on environmental, social, and governance (ESG) issues, the role of regulators and government in ESG investing is becoming more important. As a result, ESG investing, which involves investing in companies that prioritize these issues, is gaining popularity as investors seek to align their values with their investments. However, the regulatory framework for ESG investing is still evolving, and government policies and initiatives significantly shape the industry. In this chapter, we will explore the regulatory framework for ESG investing, government policies and initiatives promoting ESG investing, and the influence of global regulatory developments on ESG investing.

## The Regulatory Framework for ESG Investing

As environmental, social, and governance (ESG) investing continues to expand, the regulatory framework surrounding it is also evolving to keep pace. While there may not be a universally accepted definition of ESG investing, it is clear that the principles and guidelines developed by regulators in various countries are becoming increasingly crucial.

In the European Union, for example, the European Commission has been working to promote sustainable finance through various initiatives and regulations, including the Taxonomy Regulation, which provides a framework for classifying environmentally sustainable economic activities. Similarly, in the United States, the SEC has issued guidance on how companies can disclose their ESG risks and opportunities.

These guidelines and regulations are important for ensuring the **transparency and reliability** of ESG investing for investors and promoting consistency across the industry. In addition, they help to ensure that companies are held accountable for their ESG performance and that investors can make informed decisions about where to allocate their capital.

It is, therefore, important for market participants to stay informed about the regulatory developments in the ESG investing space, as it is likely to continue to shape the industry in the future.


### Government Policies and Initiatives Promoting ESG Investing

Governments worldwide increasingly recognize the importance of promoting environmentally and socially responsible investing, also known as ESG investing. In addition to creating a regulatory framework that supports ESG investing, governments are also implementing various policies and initiatives to encourage this investing. These policies can take many forms, such as tax incentives, grants, and subsidies.

One example of a government promoting ESG investing is the United Kingdom. The UK government has introduced several measures to encourage ESG investing, including creating the Green Investment Bank. This institution is designed to fund projects that promote environmental sustainability, such as renewable energy and low-carbon transportation. The UK government has also established the Green Bonds Market, which allows companies and organizations to issue bonds specifically earmarked for environmental projects.

Similarly, in the United States, the government has also taken steps to promote ESG investing. One example of this is the establishment of the Green Bank, which provides funding for clean energy projects. The US also has a Green Bond Market, which works similarly to the UK Green Bonds Market.

Overall, government policies and initiatives play an important role in promoting ESG investing by creating a supportive environment for these investments. Investors need to be aware of the different incentives and programs available to them, as these can make a significant difference in the long-term financial performance of their investments.

*A stern-faced government official.*

## The Influence of Global Regulatory Developments on ESG Investing

The impact of global regulatory developments on environmental, social, and governance (ESG) investing is of increasing importance as the popularity and growth of ESG investing continue to rise. The proliferation of ESG investing, which focuses on investing in companies that positively impact environmental and social issues, in addition to traditional financial considerations, has led to a growing need for clear and consistent guidelines and standards for responsible investing.

In response to this need, various international organizations and governing bodies have developed principles and guidelines for responsible investing. One notable example is the United Nations, which has established the Principles for Responsible Investment (PRI), a set of six principles that provide a framework for responsible investing and promote the integration of ESG considerations into investment decision-making. The PRI aims to encourage the adoption of responsible investing practices worldwide and has been adopted by many investors and investment managers.

Another important global regulatory development in sustainable finance is the Financial Stability Board's (FSB) Task Force on Climate-related Financial Disclosures (TCFD). The TCFD has developed a set of recommendations for the disclosure of climate-related financial information, which guides companies on disclosing the potential financial impacts of climate-related risks and opportunities in their financial filings. The TCFD's recommendations are designed to **promote transparency and consistency** in the disclosure of climate-related financial information and are expected to play a key role in helping investors and other stakeholders to understand better and manage the financial risks and opportunities associated with climate change.

In addition to the PRI and TCFD, various other global regulatory developments are shaping the ESG investing industry. For example, the European Union has implemented regulations that require companies to disclose their non-financial information, including their ESG performance, in their annual reports. The Securities and Exchange Commission (SEC) in the United States has also issued guidance on disclosing ESG information by public companies. In addition, various countries and regions have also implemented their guidelines and regulations for responsible investing.

Overall, global regulatory developments significantly shape the ESG investing industry and influence how ESG considerations are integrated into investment decision-making. These developments will continue to shape the industry in the future. Investors and other stakeholders must stay informed about the latest regulatory developments and their implications for the ESG investing industry.


In conclusion, the role of regulators and government in ESG investing is becoming increasingly important as the industry grows. The regulatory framework for ESG investing is still evolving, but it is becoming increasingly important as the industry grows. Government policies and initiatives play an important role in promoting ESG investing, and global regulatory developments also significantly influence the industry. As ESG investing continues to grow in popularity, the regulatory framework and government policies will likely continue to evolve to meet the needs of investors and the industry.

## Chapter Summary

- The role of regulators and government in ESG investing is becoming increasingly important.
- A regulatory framework for ESG investing is evolving, with guidelines and regulations from the European Commission and the SEC in the US.
- Governments are implementing various policies and initiatives to encourage ESG investing, such as tax incentives, grants, and subsidies.
- The UN has established the Principles for Responsible Investment (PRI) to provide a framework for responsible investing.
- The Financial Stability Board's (FSB) Task Force on Climate-related Financial Disclosures (TCFD) has developed a set of recommendations for the disclosure of climate-related financial information.
- The European Union has implemented regulations that require companies to disclose their non-financial information, including their ESG performance, in their annual reports.
- The SEC in the US has issued guidance on disclosing ESG information by public companies.
- Global regulatory developments significantly shape the ESG investing industry and will continue to do so in the future.

# 7

## ESG INVESTING AND FINANCIAL PERFORMANCE

E SG investing, which stands for environmental, social, and governance investing, is a rapidly growing field that has gained significant attention in recent years. ESG investing involves investing in companies with strong environmental, social, and governance practices. This chapter will examine the historical and current research on the relationship between ESG and financial performance, the potential risks and benefits of ESG investing for investors, and the role of active management in ESG investing.

### The Historical and Current Research on the Relationship Between ESG and Financial Performance

The study of environmental, social, and governance (ESG) factors and financial performance has been a topic of interest for many years. Historically, there has been a diverse body of evidence regarding the correlation between ESG and financial performance. However, in recent years, many studies have revealed a **positive relationship** between companies prioritizing ESG factors and their financial performance.

A study conducted by the Morgan Stanley Institute for Sustainable Investing found that companies with strong environmental, social, and governance (ESG) practices tend to have higher returns and lower volatility than their peers. Companies that prioritize ESG factors may be better equipped to identify and manage potential risks and capitalize on opportunities. Furthermore, these companies are more likely to have sound management, which is an important factor in achieving long-term financial performance. The study highlights that ESG practices are not just a matter of corporate responsibility. Still, they also directly impact a company's bottom line. Companies prioritizing ESG factors are more likely to have a sustainable business model, which is crucial in today's business environment. Investing in companies that have strong ESG practices can be a smart financial decision, as they are more likely to be resilient in the face of economic challenges and are better positioned to capitalize on growth opportunities in the long run.

Another study conducted by the Harvard Business Review found that companies with strong ESG practices tend to have better employee engagement and retention. This is because employees felt more connected to and invested in a company that positively impacted the world. Additionally, these companies tend to have a stronger brand and reputation, which can lead to increased customer loyalty and better business performance.

Furthermore, companies that prioritize ESG factors are more likely to be viewed as leaders in their industry, and this perception can lead to increased market share and revenue growth. This is because consumers are becoming increasingly conscious of the impact of their purchasing decisions on the environment and society, and they are more likely to support companies that align with their values.

The studies suggest that investing in companies with strong ESG practices is more than a socially responsible decision. Still, it can also be a financially savvy one. These companies are better equipped to manage risks, capitalize on opportunities, and achieve long-term financial performance. They also tend to have engaged employees, a strong brand, and a reputation for leadership in their industry, all of which contribute to their overall success.

This research supports the idea that incorporating ESG factors into investment decisions can improve long-term financial outcomes. It also highlights the importance of considering ESG factors as a potential indicator of a company's overall health and future potential. As more and more investors and organizations begin to recognize the importance of ESG factors in driving financial performance, incorporating ESG considerations into investment decisions will likely continue to gain traction.

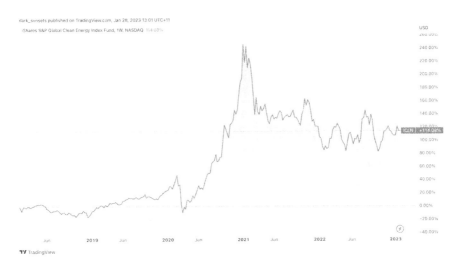

*iShares S&P Global Clean Energy Index Fund 5 year chart showing a +114% return.*
*Source: TradingView*

## The Potential Risks and Benefits of ESG Investing for Investors

Regarding ESG investing, it's important to consider both the potential risks and benefits for investors. ESG investing has gained significant attention in recent years as more and more investors are becoming aware of the impact that their investments can have on the world.

On the one hand, investing in companies that prioritize and adhere to strong ESG practices can lead to higher returns and lower volatility. This is because companies prioritizing sustainability tend to be more resilient and better able to navigate economic challenges, which can lead to more stable returns for investors. Additionally, companies with strong ESG practices may be more attractive to consumers and employees, leading to long-term growth and success.

However, companies may also need to be **more transparent** about their ESG practices. This could lead to investing in companies that are not truly sustainable or only paying lip service to the concept of sustainability without actually implementing meaningful change. Furthermore, some investors may be concerned that ESG investing may lead to lower returns than traditional investing, as companies may have to divert resources toward sustainability initiatives rather than growth and expansion.

In conclusion, while ESG investing presents potential risks and benefits for investors, it's important to consider both sides of the equation when making investment decisions. Investors should conduct thorough research and due diligence to invest in sustainable companies committed to positively impacting the world.

## The Role of Active Management in ESG Investing

The importance of active management in environmental, social, and governance (ESG) investing cannot be overstated. Active managers take on the task of thoroughly researching and handpicking companies with a demonstrated commitment to strong ESG practices. This process involves evaluating a wide range of criteria, such as a company's environmental impact, treatment of employees, and governance structure, to ensure that they align with the values and principles of ESG investing.

In addition to the initial selection process, active managers also play a vital role in monitoring and engaging with the companies in which they have invested. This **ongoing engagement is crucial** as it allows them to stay informed about changes in a company's ESG practices and act accordingly. For example, suppose a company previously considered a leader in sustainable practices were to decrease its efforts in this area suddenly. In that case, active managers could detect this shift and decide whether to continue investing in the company.

Furthermore, active management can help investors ensure that the companies they invest in are committed to sustainability and not just paying lip service to the ESG movement. With active management, investors can have greater confidence that their money is being directed toward companies truly working to impact the world positively.

Ultimately, active management plays a crucial role in the ESG investing process. Through thorough research, ongoing monitoring, and engagement, active managers can identify and invest in companies that are truly committed to sustainable practices, providing investors with peace of mind that their money is being directed toward companies that align with their values.

In conclusion, ESG investing is a rapidly growing field that has recently gained significant attention. The research on the relationship between ESG and financial performance has found evidence of a positive relationship between the two. However, there are potential risks and benefits to ESG investing that investors should be aware of. Active management plays a crucial role in ESG investing by researching and selecting companies with strong ESG practices and monitoring and engaging with the companies in which they invest to ensure that they continue to meet the ESG criteria.

**Chapter Summary**

- ESG investing involves investing in companies with strong environmental, social, and governance practices.
- Studies have revealed a positive relationship between companies prioritizing ESG factors and their financial performance.
- Investing in companies that prioritize and adhere to strong ESG practices can lead to higher returns and lower volatility.
- ESG investing presents potential risks and benefits for investors. Therefore, when making investment decisions, it is important to consider both sides of the equation.
- Active management plays a crucial role in ESG investing by researching and selecting companies with strong ESG practices and monitoring and engaging with the companies in which they invest.
- Active management can help investors ensure that the companies they invest in are committed to sustainability and not just paying lip service to the ESG movement.

- Through thorough research, ongoing monitoring, and engagement, active managers can identify and invest in companies that are truly committed to sustainable practices.
- Investors should conduct thorough research and due diligence to invest in sustainable companies committed to positively impacting the world.

# 8

## ESG INVESTING IN PRACTICE

E nvironmental, social, and governance (ESG) investing is a rapidly growing field, with more and more investors recognizing the benefits of incorporating these considerations into their investment strategies. However, the concept of ESG investing can be complex and difficult to implement in practice. This chapter will explore the practical aspects of ESG investing, including case studies of successful ESG investing strategies, best practices for implementing ESG investing in different asset classes and investment styles, and the role of investors, asset managers, and other stakeholders in advancing ESG investing.

### Case Studies of Successful ESG Investing Strategies

The importance of environmental, social, and governance (ESG) investing has grown significantly in recent years as more and more investors recognize the potential benefits of investing in companies that prioritize sustainable practices and ethical governance. One of the best ways to understand the practical aspects of ESG investing is to look at real-world examples of successful strategies. In this section, we will explore three case studies of successful ESG investing strategies that have demonstrated the financial potential of investing in companies with strong ESG practices.

**Case Study 1: Calvert Research and Management**

Calvert Research and Management is a highly respected, well-established sustainable, responsible investment solutions provider. With over 40 years of experience in the industry, they have developed a reputation for excellence in ESG-integrated portfolio management.

At the core of Calvert's investment philosophy is a deep commitment to environmental sustainability, social responsibility, and corporate governance. As a result, they take a comprehensive and holistic approach to evaluating companies' performance, carefully analyzing their environmental practices and governance structures to identify firms that are best positioned to create long-term value for all stakeholders.

To achieve this goal, Calvert employs a rigorous research and analysis process incorporating a wide range of data and metrics. For example, they carefully review companies' environmental performance, assessing their energy usage, carbon emissions, water management, and other critical factors. They also evaluate companies' governance practices, looking at factors such as board composition, executive compensation, and transparency.

Through this process, Calvert can identify those companies that are truly committed to sustainable and responsible business practices. They then use this information to create tailored portfolios to meet their client's specific needs and goals. Whether through impact investing, ESG integration, or sustainable portfolio construction, Calvert's goal is to help investors achieve their financial objectives while positively impacting the world.

Calvert Research and Management has a proven track record of delivering outstanding performance with its ESG-integrated portfolios. One of the key indicators of this success is the consistent outperformance of their portfolios compared to their benchmarks. For example, over the last decade, ending December 2022, the Calvert Environmental Solutions Fund has demonstrated exceptional returns, delivering an annualized return of 14.26%. This performance compares favorably to the Russell

1000 Growth Index benchmark, which returned 14.09% annualized over the same period.

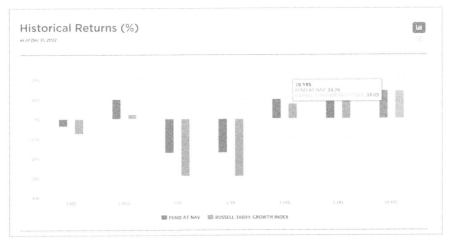

Historical Returns (%)
as of Dec 31, 2022

10 YRS
FUND AT NAV: 14.26
RUSSELL 1000% GROWTH INDEX: 14.09

FUND AT NAV    RUSSELL 1000% GROWTH INDEX

*A series of bar charts highlighting Calvert Research and Management's positive historical returns over ten years. Source: Calvert Research and Management*

This consistent outperformance is a testament to Calvert's expertise and commitment to integrating environmental, social, and governance (ESG) factors into the investment process. By carefully researching and analyzing companies' environmental performance and governance practices, Calvert can identify those well-positioned firms to create long-term value for stakeholders. By including these companies in their portfolios, Calvert can generate returns that are competitive with traditional investments while positively impacting the world.

Furthermore, Calvert's approach to ESG integration is not limited to a single investment strategy or fund. Instead, Calvert's expertise in ESG integration can be found across their entire product line, from impact investing to sustainable portfolio construction, allowing investors to align their investment goals with their values.

In conclusion, Calvert Research and Management has a long history of delivering strong performance with its ESG-integrated portfolios. The consistent outperformance of the Calvert Environmental Solutions Fund compared to its benchmark is just one example of the company's ability to deliver strong returns while positively impacting the world. Investors looking to align their financial goals with their values can be confident that Calvert's expertise in ESG integration will help them achieve their objectives.

**Case Study 2: Impax Asset Management**

Impax Asset Management is a highly respected and accomplished global investment manager focusing on investing in companies actively working towards building a more sustainable economy. Their approach to investing is grounded in a comprehensive examination of a company's environmental, social, and governance (ESG) performance.

To ensure that they are making informed investment decisions, Impax has developed a proprietary rating system that allows them to evaluate companies on a wide range of ESG factors. These factors include but are not limited to, a company's carbon emissions, water usage, and labor practices. This system enables Impax to identify companies that are truly committed to sustainability and are making meaningful progress in this area. By investing in these companies, Impax can generate strong returns for its clients and contribute to the transition to a more sustainable economy.

Impax Asset Management has consistently demonstrated that its approach to investing, which integrates environmental, social, and governance (ESG) considerations, can generate strong returns for its clients. With £35 billion of assets under management, they generated £72.6 million profit before tax in the year ending 2021. However, the true value of Impax's approach to investing goes beyond financial returns. The company's commitment to ESG investing practices has had a tangible positive impact on the world around us. Impax is helping to drive the transition to a more sustainable economy by carefully selecting companies with a strong track record of responsible environmental and social practices. Additionally, by engaging with companies on ESG issues and encouraging them to improve their practices, Impax is helping to create a more responsible business environment.

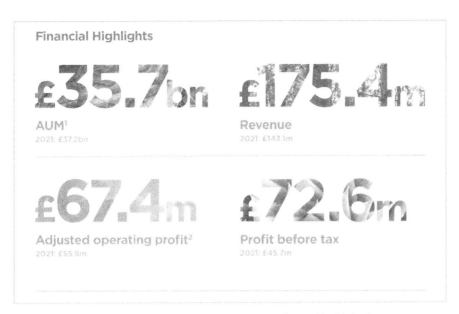

**Financial Highlights**

£35.7bn
AUM[1]
2021: £37.2bn

£175.4m
Revenue
2021: £143.1m

£67.4m
Adjusted operating profit[2]
2021: £55.8m

£72.6m
Profit before tax
2021: £45.7m

*A figure describing Impax Asset Management's positive financial highlights from 2021.*
*Source: Impax Asset Management*

In conclusion, Impax's ESG-integrated approach to investing has not only generated strong returns for its clients but also played a role in creating a more sustainable and responsible business environment. The company's commitment to ESG investing practices has been a key driver of its long-term success and has made a meaningful positive impact on the world.

### Case Study 3: Vanguard ESG U.S. Stock ETF

ESGV stands for Vanguard ESG U.S. Stock ETF, an exchange-traded fund (ETF) that aims to track the performance of companies selected based on environmental, social, and governance (ESG) criteria. ESG investing is socially responsible investing focusing on companies that positively impact the environment, society, and governance. The ETF is a way to invest in a diversified portfolio of companies that meet these criteria rather than having to select individual stocks.

Vanguard incorporates ESG practices into its ETF by using a proprietary process to screen and select the companies included in the fund. This process involves evaluating companies based on ESG criteria, such as their environmental impact, labor practices, and corporate governance. Companies that score well on these criteria are more likely to be included in the fund. In contrast, those that score poorly may be excluded or given a lower weighting in the portfolio. Vanguard also uses data from external research providers. In addition, it engages with companies through voting and engagement activities to ensure they meet the standards.

| | 1-yr | 3-yr | 5-yr | 10-yr | Since inception 09/18/2018 |
|---|---|---|---|---|---|
| ESGV (Market price) | -24.05% | 20.70% | – | – | 38.88% |
| ESGV (NAV) | -24.02% | 20.74% | – | – | 38.90% |
| Benchmark[1] | -23.99% | 21.04% | – | – | – |

*A table with Vanguard's ESGV ETF returns over a 1, 3, 5, and ten year period. Source: Vanguard*

Vanguard's ESG U.S. Stock ETF, like other funds that focus on socially responsible investing, has slightly lower returns than its benchmark (FTSE US All Cap Choice Index), demonstrating a 20.70% compared to the benchmark's 21.04% over three years. This is because the fund is selecting companies based on a set of ESG criteria, which may exclude some companies with higher financial returns but do not meet the criteria for ESG investing.

However, the slightly lower returns may be offset by the positive impact that the fund's ESG investment strategy can have on the world around us. By investing in companies that are committed to environmental and social responsibility, the fund can help promote sustainable business practices and contribute to the development of a more sustainable economy. Additionally, by avoiding companies that engage in unethical or environmentally harmful practices, the fund can help reduce the negative impact of these practices on society and the planet.

In summary, while Vanguard's ESG U.S. Stock ETF may have slightly lower returns compared to some benchmark indexes, it is important to consider the positive impact of the fund's ESG investment strategy on the world around us.

## Best Practices for Implementing ESG Investing

ESG (environmental, social, and governance) investing is a growing trend in finance, as more and more investors are becoming conscious of their investments' environmental and social impact. This form of investing focuses on companies with strong environmental, social, and governance practices and working towards sustainability. To successfully navigate the world of ESG investing, it is important to understand the key principles and best practices. This section will discuss five of the most important best practices for ESG investing, including understanding the companies you are investing in, diversifying your investments, considering the long-term, engaging with companies, and monitoring and assessing your investments.

### Understand the Companies You Are Investing In

Understanding the companies you are investing in is one of the most important aspects of ESG investing. Before investing, it is crucial to conduct thorough research and due diligence on the company to understand its exposure to environmental, social, and governance (ESG) risks. This research should include evaluating the company's environmental impact, labor practices, and corporate governance structure. By understanding the company's ESG risks and opportunities, investors can make informed decisions about whether or not to invest and how to engage with the company to encourage positive change.

When evaluating a company's environmental impact, it is important to consider factors such as its carbon footprint, energy usage, and water consumption. Investors should also look at the company's efforts to reduce their environmental impact and their plans for addressing climate change. Additionally, investors should assess the company's labor practices, including their treatment of employees and their efforts to promote diversity, equity, and inclusion in the workplace.

Corporate governance is another important aspect when evaluating a company's ESG risks. Investors should look at the company's leadership and management structure, including their board of directors and executive leadership team. They should also assess the company's transparency, accountability, and commitment to ethical business practices. By understanding the company's corporate governance structure, investors can identify any potential red flags or areas for improvement.

In conclusion, understanding the companies you invest in is a key aspect of ESG investing. By evaluating the company's environmental impact, labor practices, and corporate governance structure, investors can identify the company's ESG risks and opportunities and make informed decisions about whether or not to invest and how to engage with the company to encourage positive change.

**Diversify Your Investments**

One of the key investing principles is diversification, which is the strategy of spreading your investments across various sectors, industries, and geographies. The idea behind this is to reduce the overall risk of your portfolio by not putting all of your eggs in one basket.

This is especially important when investing in companies that align with environmental, social, and governance (ESG) criteria. ESG investing involves investing in companies with strong corporate governance practices that positively impact the environment and society.

However, it's important to note that not all companies or sectors are created equal regarding ESG risks. For example, companies in the oil and gas sector may be more exposed to environmental risks than those in the renewable energy sector. Similarly, companies in the consumer goods sector may be more exposed to human rights risks than those in the healthcare sector.

By diversifying your investments across different sectors and industries, you can reduce the overall risk of your portfolio and increase your chances of achieving long-term financial success. Additionally, by investing in companies across different geographies, you can reduce your portfolio risk by not relying too heavily on any one country or region.

In summary, diversifying your investments is a crucial strategy for reducing overall portfolio risk, especially in ESG investing. It's important to consider the specific ESG risks associated with different sectors and industries and to invest in various companies across different geographies to minimize risk.

. . .

## Consider the Long-Term

Adopting a long-term perspective on environmental, social, and governance (ESG) investing is essential. This is because the benefits of ESG investing may not be immediately apparent and may take several years to materialize fully. Therefore, it is crucial to focus on a company's long-term potential and ability to effectively manage and navigate the various ESG risks it may face rather than just its short-term performance.

To ensure that a company is well-positioned to meet the evolving demands of responsible investing, it is important to consider its track record and commitment to ESG principles. It is also important to assess the company's plans for the future to ensure that it is taking steps to address any potential ESG risks and opportunities.

*A wise old owl perched atop a towering oak tree deep in thought.*

Furthermore, it is also important to consider the broader societal and environmental trends that may impact a company's long-term success. For example, the increasing focus on sustainability and shifting towards a low-carbon economy will likely significantly impact many industries.

Therefore, considering how a company is positioning itself to navigate these challenges.

Overall, taking a long-term perspective on ESG investing is crucial for achieving the fullest potential of your investment. It is important to consider a company's current performance, long-term potential, and ability to adapt to the changing landscape of responsible investing. By taking a long-term view and carefully evaluating a company's ESG risks and opportunities, investors can make more informed decisions and increase the chances of achieving their desired investment outcomes.

### Engage With Companies

As a shareholder, you can play a crucial role in promoting environmental, social, and governance (ESG) practices within the companies you invest in. One effective way to do this is by actively engaging with the companies.

One way to engage with companies is by participating in shareholder meetings and casting your vote on proposals related to ESG issues. This can include voting on resolutions related to environmental impact, labor rights, and ethical business practices. Using your voting power as a shareholder, you can help influence the company's direction and push for more sustainable and responsible practices.

Another way to engage with companies is communicating directly with management and board members. This can include sending letters or emails, attending town hall meetings, or setting up one-on-one meetings. By communicating directly with the company's people, you can share your concerns and suggestions for improving ESG practices. You can also ask questions and seek clarification on the company's current policies and plans.

Finally, you can join or form shareholder groups focused on ESG issues. These groups are made up of shareholders who share similar concerns and goals. Together, these shareholders can take collective action, such as filing shareholder resolutions, organizing campaigns and events, and engaging with other stakeholders. By joining or forming a shareholder group, you can amplify your voice and work with others to drive change within the company.

In summary, you can encourage companies to improve their ESG practices as a shareholder. You can vote on ESG-related proposals by engaging with companies, communicating directly with management and board members, and joining or forming shareholder groups focused on ESG issues. Together, these actions can help to create a more sustainable and responsible business environment.

## Monitor and Assess Your Investments

Properly monitoring and assessing your investments is paramount if you wish to ensure that they align with your environmental, social, and governance (ESG) values and goals. This process involves a variety of tasks, such as tracking the performance of the companies in which you have invested on ESG issues, evaluating any changes in the leadership or business strategy of these companies, and staying informed about any material events or developments that may impact the ESG risk profile of the company.

For example, you should monitor the companies' adherence to environmental regulations, labor rights policies, and approaches to corporate governance. Investors can do this by keeping an eye on their annual reports, sustainability reports, and other relevant documents. You should also pay attention to any news or developments that may impact the company's reputation, such as lawsuits, scandals, or major management changes.

Furthermore, keeping track of changes in the company's leadership, business strategy, and overall financial performance is important. For instance, a change in the CEO or the company's board of directors may impact the company's ESG performance. Similarly, if the company announces a major acquisition or divestiture, it may affect its ESG risk profile.

Finally, it is essential to know material events or developments that may impact the company's ESG risk profile. For instance, a natural disaster, a change in government regulations, or a major industry disruption may significantly impact the company's performance and ESG risks.

Monitoring and assessing your investments regularly is crucial for ensuring they align with your ESG values and goals. By keeping track of the companies' performance on ESG issues, evaluating any changes in the company's leadership or business strategy, and being aware of any material events or developments that may impact the company's ESG risk profile, you can make informed decisions and optimize your portfolio.

In conclusion, ESG investing is a crucial aspect of responsible investing, focusing on companies that align with environmental, social, and governance criteria. It is important to understand the companies you are investing in by conducting thorough research and due diligence on the company's environmental impact, labor practices, and corporate governance structure. Diversifying your investments across different sectors, industries, and geographies is a key strategy for reducing overall portfolio risk. Additionally, adopting a long-term perspective on ESG investing is essential as the benefits may take several years to materialize fully. By following these principles, investors can make informed decisions, minimize risk, and achieve long-term financial success while promoting positive environmental and societal change.

### The Role of Investors, Asset Managers, and Other Stakeholders in Advancing ESG Investing

The advancement of environmental, social, and governance (ESG) investing is a collective effort that involves multiple stakeholders. Investors, as the primary drivers of the capital market, play a crucial role in promoting ESG investing. By incorporating ESG factors into their investment decisions, they are signaling to companies that robust ESG practices are not only socially responsible but also financially beneficial.

Asset managers also play a vital role in advancing ESG investing by providing products and services that cater to the growing demand for sustainable investing. They can offer investment options that align with the values and goals of socially conscious investors and also help to educate them about the benefits of ESG investing.

Regulators also significantly advance ESG investing by creating a supportive framework that promotes transparency, disclosure, and accountability for ESG performance. They can also establish standards and guidelines that ensure companies are held accountable for their ESG performance.

Non-governmental organizations (NGOs) also play an important role in advancing ESG investing by providing education, resources, and advocacy for sustainable investing. In addition, they can work with investors and asset managers to raise awareness about the benefits of ESG investing and help shape policy and regulatory frameworks that support sustainable investing.

Overall, advancing ESG investing requires the collective effort of investors, asset managers, regulators, and NGOs. Each stakeholder is critical in promoting sustainable investing and creating a more responsible and sustainable capital market.

In conclusion, ESG investing is a complex and rapidly growing field. Still, by understanding the practical aspects of ESG investing, investors can meaningfully incorporate these considerations into their investment strategies. This chapter has explored case studies of successful ESG investing strategies, best practices for implementing ESG investing in different asset classes and investment styles, and the role of investors, asset managers, and other stakeholders in advancing ESG investing. By understanding these aspects, investors can make more informed and sustainable investment decisions.

## Chapter Summary

- ESG investing is a rapidly growing field, with more and more investors recognizing the potential benefits of incorporating these considerations into their investment strategies.
- Case studies of successful ESG investing strategies demonstrate the financial potential of investing in companies with strong ESG practices.
- Understanding the companies, you are investing in is a key aspect of ESG investing.

- Diversifying your investments is a crucial strategy for reducing overall portfolio risk, especially in ESG investing.
- Adopting a long-term perspective when it comes to ESG investing is essential.
- As a shareholder, you can play a crucial role in promoting ESG practices within the companies you invest in by engaging with them.
- Properly monitoring and assessing your investments is paramount if you wish to ensure that they align with your ESG values and goals.
- The advancement of ESG investing is a collective effort that involves multiple stakeholders, including investors, asset managers, regulators, and NGOs.

# EPILOGUE

In conclusion, ESG investing has become an increasingly important topic in the investment community. By considering environmental, social, and governance factors in investment decisions, investors can positively impact society and the planet and improve financial performance. This book has discussed various aspects of ESG investing, including integrating ESG considerations into investment strategy, measuring and evaluating ESG performance, and understanding the role of regulators and government in ESG investing. Additionally, we have explored the relationship between ESG investing and financial performance and practical examples of ESG investing in practice. Overall, it is clear that ESG investing is a complex and evolving field. Still, by understanding the key principles and best practices outlined in this book, investors can make informed decisions that align with their values and financial goals.

## The Benefits of ESG Investing for Sustainability and Positive Impact

Integrating environmental, social, and governance (ESG) considerations into investment decisions is crucial for achieving sustainable financial returns and promoting positive social and environmental change. ESG investing is a holistic approach that looks beyond traditional financial metrics to assess the long-term sustainability of a company or organization.

By considering ESG factors, investors can identify potential risks and opportunities that may not be visible through traditional financial analysis. This can lead to a more diversified and resilient investment portfolio, better equipped to navigate the complex and rapidly changing business landscape.

Furthermore, ESG investing is a powerful tool for promoting positive social and environmental change. By directing investment capital towards companies and organizations that prioritize sustainability, investors can play a key role in driving the transition towards a more just and sustainable society.

In addition, research has shown that companies with strong ESG performance tend to have better risk-adjusted returns and higher growth potential than their peers. This is because companies with sustainable business practices are more likely to be able to adapt and thrive in an uncertain future.

In conclusion, ESG investing is not only a responsible and ethical approach to investing but also a practical and profitable one. By considering ESG factors, investors can achieve sustainable financial returns while promoting positive social and environmental change.

## The Ongoing Evolution of ESG Investing and Future Opportunities for Growth

Environmental, social, and governance (ESG) investing has undergone significant evolution in recent years and is expected to continue growing. ESG investing is an approach to investment that considers the impact of a company or organization on the environment, society, and corporate governance when making investment decisions.

The ongoing evolution of ESG investing has been driven by a growing awareness of the need to address pressing social and environmental issues, such as climate change and inequality, as well as a recognition that companies with strong ESG performance tend to have better risk-adjusted returns and higher growth potential.

One of the key trends in ESG investing is the increasing demand for data and transparency. Investors seek more information on how companies manage ESG risks and opportunities. Companies are responding by providing more ESG-related data and disclosures.

Another trend is the growing interest in impact investing, which focuses on investing in companies and organizations working to achieve specific social or environmental outcomes. Impact investing is an effective way for investors to align their values and financial goals. As a result, it is expected to continue growing in popularity.

ESG investing also has future opportunities for growth as many investors have an increased understanding of the materiality of ESG issues on their investment portfolios and its potential impact on long-term returns. As a result, more institutional investors are incorporating ESG factors into their investment decisions. Moreover, there is growing pressure from stakeholders, such as governments and consumers, for companies to improve their ESG performance.

In conclusion, ESG investing is an ongoing evolution, and the field is expected to grow. As investors become more aware of the materiality of ESG issues in their portfolios, they become more interested in incorporating ESG considerations into their investment decisions. This trend is expected to continue, providing more opportunities for growth in the ESG investing space.

# ACKNOWLEDGMENTS

Writing a book is a journey; I could not have done it alone. So I want to express my deepest gratitude to the many people who have helped me along the way.

First and foremost, I would like to thank my family for their unwavering support and encouragement throughout the writing of this book. Their love and patience have been a constant source of inspiration; I could not have done this without them.

I also extend my deepest gratitude to my mentor Justina, whose guidance and wisdom have been invaluable in shaping my understanding of ESG investing. His insights and expertise have been instrumental in the development of this book.

I am also grateful to the team at Book Bound Studios for their support and guidance throughout the publishing process. The cover and interior design work provided by the team were amazing and exceeded my expectations.

I would also like to thank the many experts and practitioners in the field of ESG investing who have shared their time and knowledge with me. Their insights and experiences have been invaluable in the development of this book.

Finally, thank you, the reader, for your interest in this topic. I hope this book will be a valuable resource for those looking to understand and implement ESG strategies in their investment decisions.

# ABOUT THE AUTHOR

Robert Buckley is a financial professional with over 15 years of experience in the industry. He is a specialist in ESG Investing and has spent the past decade researching and studying the field. He has held various positions in the investment management sector, including portfolio management, research, and strategy development.

Robert is passionate about promoting sustainable and responsible investing and is dedicated to helping investors understand the benefits and risks of incorporating ESG factors in their investment decisions. He believes that by considering ESG factors, investors can achieve both financial returns and positively impact the world.

Robert enjoys hiking, reading, and spending time with his family in his free time.

# $10.99 FREE EBOOK

**Receive Your Free Copy of The Power of Intelligent Investing**

Or visit:
bookboundstudios.wixsite.com/robert-buckley

Made in United States
North Haven, CT
23 August 2023

40683296R00055